The Dynamic Companies

When change is the only norm.

Forward

This book offers a concise reflection, drawing from personal observations and insights derived from a doctoral dissertation in change management. The findings suggest that certain companies inherently possess a "change DNA," seamlessly integrating adaptability into their organizational fabric due to the nature of their business. In contrast, other companies must take a more deliberate approach, utilizing both scientific and social strategies to successfully implement change. The book explores these dynamics, providing valuable lessons for organizations navigating the complexities of change.

M. G. Maraee, MSM, DBA

2024

Disclaimer:

This book is a based on a theory stemming from personal research and observations and more research is needed to support this theory.

Contents

- Organizational Culture of Change and Change Management Theory 5
- Companies Where Change is Part of the Culture 5
- Change Management Theories 6
- The Intersection of Daily Norms of Change and Formal Change Management 7
- Organizational Flexibility vs. Strategic Alignment 8
- Discovering an Ingrained Culture of Change 10
- Transformational Leadership and Change Resistance 10
- The Unexpected Discovery: Change as a Constant 11
- A Deeper Look at Companies with Change-Driven DNA 12
- Revisiting Change Management Theories in Light of This Discovery 14
- Transformational Leadership in Dynamic Environments 15
- The Role of Employee Empowerment in Change-Driven Cultures 16
- Implications for the Manufacturing Industry 16
- The Perceived Relationship with Change Leaders and its Impact on Readiness for Change 17
- The Importance of Trust in the Change Process 18
- Effective communication: A Cornerstone for Building Relationships. 20
- Empowerment and Involvement in the Change Process 21
- The Role of Authentic Leadership in Strengthening Relationships 22
- Impact on Organizational Readiness for Change 23
- Adaptation as the Norm 24
- The Culture of Continuous Innovation 25
- Frequent New Projects and Their Impact on Employee Mindsets 26
- Collaborative Work Environments and Change Acceptance 27
- Leadership's Role in Cultivating Change-Ready Employees 28
- The Benefits of a Change-Accepting Workforce 30
- In Concussion 31

Organizational Culture of Change and Change Management Theory

Change is inevitable in any organization. It occurs in different forms—through product innovation, market diversification, technological shifts, or organizational restructuring. Some companies have conscientiously embedded change into their culture, making it a part of their daily operations while others deal with change as part of their norm. This approach contrasts with the more structured methods of formal change management, which is often reactive and implemented as a response to specific events. Exploring companies where change is a norm and comparing their practices to established change management theories can shed light on the nuances of managing change. Furthermore, few studies address the issue of whether the daily handling of change in companies that offer diverse products and services affects the organization's ability to manage larger, planned changes.

Companies Where Change is Part of the Culture

Some companies have developed organizational cultures where change is not seen as a disruption but a core element of their business operations. These companies, typically in fast-paced industries such as technology, retail, and media, thrive on continuous adaptation. Take, for example, Amazon. Known for its innovation in e-commerce, cloud computing, and logistics, Amazon integrates change into its culture by encouraging experimentation, calculated risk-taking, and rapid decision-making. This is also reflected in its famous leadership principles, which prioritize customer obsession, ownership, and the willingness to change course when needed. Another prime example is Google, where constant innovation in both product development and operational structure is the norm. Google's work culture embraces change at every level, from agile project management to promoting creative freedom in the workplace. Employees are encouraged to test new ideas without fear of failure, and teams often pivot projects in response to emerging trends, customer feedback, or new technologies. Change at Google is more than just a response to external factors; it is woven into the fabric of how the company operates daily. In fact, Google's ability to eliminate a product and start another is another great example of their agile approach to change. The driving force behind these companies is their ability to harness change as a mechanism for growth and competitive advantage. Unlike organizations that see change as a project to be managed, these companies have developed mechanisms for continuously absorbing and responding to changes. Their internal processes, from decision-making to team collaboration, are designed to accommodate fluidity.

Change Management Theories

Contrasting these daily, culture-driven adaptations are formal change management theories, which often emphasize planned, structured approaches to dealing with change. Two dominant models in change management theory are Kurt Lewin's Change Management Model and John Kotter's 8-Step Process for Leading Change.

Kurt Lewin's model suggests that change occurs in three stages: Unfreeze, Change, and Refreeze. In the "Unfreeze" stage, the organization must prepare itself to accept change by recognizing the need for it and challenging the existing status quo. The "Change" stage involves the transition itself, which often brings uncertainty and resistance from employees. Finally, in the "Refreeze" stage, the changes are solidified, and the organization returns to a state of equilibrium, adopting new behaviors and processes.

On the other hand, Kotter's 8-Step Process is more granular, emphasizing the need to create urgency, form coalitions, and develop a vision for change. His model also stresses the importance of building momentum and embedding changes into the organization's culture through strong leadership and continuous reinforcement. Both models are grounded in the idea of change as a disruption to normal operations that must be managed carefully. This contrasts sharply with companies like Amazon or Google, where change is not an exception but an expectation. Rather than unfreezing and refreezing processes, these organizations maintain a state of continuous movement and adaptation, often making the more rigid steps outlined in traditional models unnecessary or irrelevant.

The Intersection of Daily Norms of Change and Formal Change Management

One critical observation is that while many change management theories focus on how to guide an organization through planned, episodic transformations, they often overlook how organizations handle continuous, daily change. Companies with dynamic work environments and diverse product offerings must navigate a different landscape of change management. These organizations don't "freeze" or "refreeze" but instead operate in a fluid state of constant adaptation. This raises the question: does the daily handling of change—common in companies with a wide range of products or services—affect their ability to manage larger, planned changes? In organizations like Google and Amazon, employees are so accustomed to change that the shock or disruption typically associated with planned changes might be minimized. The mindset and structures for adapting to change are already in place, allowing these companies to transition more smoothly through larger strategic shifts. However, the continuous nature of change in these environments also creates a different challenge: ensuring that the broader vision and long-term goals do not get lost amid the constant movement. Few studies have explored this intersection between daily norms of change and formal change management processes. Most research focuses on managing large-scale organizational change, treating it as an extraordinary event. This leaves a gap in understanding how companies with a high tolerance for daily change respond to structured change initiatives. Do they find it easier to implement these changes due to their existing culture of flexibility? Or do they struggle to align short-term adaptations with long-term strategic changes?

Organizational Flexibility vs. Strategic Alignment

For companies that thrive on daily change, one potential issue is the risk of losing strategic alignment. In a fast-moving environment, the temptation to constantly pivot based on short-term feedback or new developments can lead to a lack of coherence in long-term strategy. While agile companies may excel at incremental innovation, there is a risk that they may struggle with deeper, more transformational changes that require long-term commitment and stability. In contrast, companies that adopt formal change management processes tend to have a clearer structure for aligning change with long-term goals. By focusing on creating a sense of urgency, building coalitions, and embedding change into the culture, models like Kotter's provide a roadmap for ensuring that large-scale changes are purposeful and aligned with the organization's vision. This contrast highlights a critical tension: companies that are too focused on continuous, short-term change may find it difficult to implement more deliberate, long-term strategic changes. Conversely, companies that rely heavily on formal change management processes may struggle to adapt to the faster pace of change in dynamic industries.

Change is an inherent part of any business, but how organizations handle it varies widely. Some companies have developed cultures where change is a daily norm, and this provides them with the flexibility to innovate and adapt rapidly. However, is this culture by any chance connected to a diversified product where change is part of the daily work? These companies may face challenges in maintaining strategic alignment amid constant movement, unless their strategy is to continue to become innovative. On the other hand, traditional change management theories, which emphasize structured, planned change, provide useful frameworks for aligning change with long-term goals but may not be well-suited for fast-paced environments. I found that the intersection of daily norms of change and formal change management processes is an area that requires further exploration. Few studies have focused on whether companies accustomed to handling daily changes due to their diverse products or practices are better equipped to manage planned changes. Understanding this dynamic could provide valuable insights for organizations seeking to balance agility with strategic coherence in an increasingly complex business environment.

Discovering an Ingrained Culture of Change

The role of leadership in managing organizational change has been a longstanding area of interest within management studies. My doctoral research, titled *"Transformational Leadership Style and Employee Resistance to Change in the Manufacturing Industry," initially focused on the relationship between leadership and employee reactions to change initiatives, particularly in manufacturing environments. The objective was to explore how transformational leadership could help reduce employee resistance during times of change. However, as the research progressed, I encountered an unexpected pattern: in some companies, change was no longer a discrete, managed event but an ingrained part of their daily operations. This realization prompted a deeper examination of how certain manufacturing companies, driven by product innovation and frequent market demands, had adopted a culture of change so deeply that traditional change management practices were nearly irrelevant.

Transformational Leadership and Change Resistance

At the outset of my research, the primary objective was to investigate the influence of transformational leadership on employee resistance to change within the manufacturing industry. Transformational leadership, with its focus on inspiring and motivating employees, seemed ideally suited for environments undergoing significant shifts. The theory posits that transformational leaders foster trust, commitment, and loyalty by creating a shared vision and encouraging employees to align with broader organizational goals. In the context of change, this leadership style was expected to mitigate resistance by engaging employees in the process and ensuring that they feel valued and understood. The research sought to answer several questions:

- How does transformational leadership influence employee attitudes toward change?

- Can transformational leadership reduce resistance to change more effectively than other leadership styles?

- What role does employee empowerment play in this process?

The hypothesis was that transformational leaders, by fostering a collaborative and visionary approach, would reduce resistance and increase employee engagement in change initiatives. This research primarily targeted companies in the advanced manufacturing sector, where operational shifts, new product lines, and process updates frequently require adjustments at all levels of the organization.

The Unexpected Discovery: Change as a Constant

During the data collection and interviews with various manufacturing companies, a surprising pattern emerged. Some organizations reported minimal resistance to change—not because of any specific leadership style, but because change had become part of their operational fabric. These companies, often involved in producing customized products or rapidly shifting product lines, saw change not as an event to be managed but as a regular occurrence.

One particular example came from a mid-sized manufacturing company that produced custom-made equipment for various industries but mostly military and defense. This company introduced new products multiple times a year to meet the demands of different clients. As a result, employees were accustomed to regular shifts in production processes, designs, and deadlines. What became clear was that these companies had built a culture where change was normalized. Employees did not resist change because it was a routine part of their work. The company had, in essence, woven change into its organizational DNA. However, isn't that what we usually call innovation?

This discovery raised new questions: How do companies where change is a constant differ from those that implement structured change initiatives? What role does leadership play in these environments, if any, in mitigating resistance to change? The traditional models of change management—such as Lewin's Unfreeze-Change-Refreeze model or Kotter's 8-Step Process—seemed almost irrelevant in such organizations. These companies did not need to "unfreeze" their processes because there was never a static state to begin with.

A Deeper Look at Companies with Change-Driven DNA

In these organizations, change was driven by the nature of the industry itself. Companies tasked with creating multiple new products every month could not afford to treat every shift as a large-scale change initiative. Instead, they had developed mechanisms to deal with change fluidly. There was no need to create a sense of urgency or to "sell" the idea of change to employees because it was already an expected part of their daily experience. In my conversations with one of these companies' group of employees, I discovered that they see it as a fun challenge to their abilities! Talk about the right person in the right place! They did not see it as chore or need for alignment, but rather whether they can utilize their intellectual and fabrication abilities to solve a problem or a challenge. It naturally became fun rather than a task. Now was it the initial selection of employees we have to thank here? This may be something to consider.

A key finding from my interviews with leaders and employees in these companies was that the leadership's role was less about managing change and more about facilitating continuous improvement. The leaders in these organizations did not focus on mitigating resistance to change because resistance was virtually non-existent. Employees had been conditioned to expect change and to see it as part of their job. The leaders still demonstrated qualities of transformational leadership, such as vision and motivation, but these qualities were applied more toward innovation and efficiency rather than managing change.

For example, in one company, the production team met weekly to discuss upcoming product designs and any required changes to the manufacturing process. These meetings were not framed as "change management" discussions, but rather as routine operational updates. Employees were empowered to suggest improvements and anticipate future changes, and the entire organization operated with a mindset of continuous evolution. This culture of adaptability eliminated much of the friction that is typically associated with organizational change. It was replaced with excitement and an opportunity to prove their individual and collective problem solving and technical capabilities.

Revisiting Change Management Theories in Light of This Discovery

Traditional change management theories, such as Kotter's model or Lewin's, are predicated on the notion that change is an isolated event that disrupts the status quo. These models emphasize the need to prepare the organization, build coalitions, communicate a vision, and eventually "refreeze" the organization into a new state. However, the companies I encountered during my research operated under a different paradigm. There was no "status quo" to disrupt because change was a constant.

In companies where change is part of the organizational culture, the idea of "freezing" processes, even temporarily, does not apply. Instead of viewing change as a distinct phase, these organizations operate in a state of continuous adaptation. This does not mean that these companies do not plan for the future or implement strategic changes, but rather that they have built the capacity to manage change fluidly and without formal, structured interventions.

This realization challenges the relevance of traditional change management frameworks for organizations that are inherently dynamic. While structured models may be useful for companies facing large-scale, one-off changes—such as mergers, acquisitions, or major restructuring—they may be less applicable in industries where change is a daily occurrence.

Transformational Leadership in Dynamic Environments

The discovery that some organizations do not need traditional change management processes does not negate the importance of leadership. In fact, transformational leadership remains crucial in these dynamic environments. The difference is that the focus of leadership shifts from managing change to fostering innovation and maintaining alignment with the organization's goals. The fact that employees tested their technical problem-solving capabilities with each new project demonstrated a lot of empowerments. A Culture than can only be created by genuinely pinnacle leadership, as John Maxwell calls it.

Transformational leaders in companies with a culture of change still play a vital role in motivating employees, creating a shared vision, and encouraging collaboration. However, their leadership is not focused on reducing resistance to change. Instead, it is focused on empowering employees to embrace continuous improvement and on guiding the organization toward long-term success despite the constant state of flux.

One of the key components of transformational leadership is the ability to inspire and motivate employees to exceed their own expectations or abilities. In a company where change is constant, this takes on a different dimension. Leaders must not only inspire employees to adapt to change but also encourage them to proactively seek out improvements and embrace new technologies and ways of working. In this context, transformational leadership helps to cultivate a mindset of adaptability and resilience.

The Role of Employee Empowerment in Change-Driven Cultures

One of the most striking aspects of the companies I encountered was the high level of employee empowerment. In organizations where change is the norm, employees are often given significant autonomy to make decisions and suggest improvements. This empowerment plays a critical role in minimizing resistance to change. When employees feel that they have control over their work environment and that their input is valued, they are less likely to resist changes that impact them.

In these companies, the leadership's role is to provide direction and support rather than to impose change from the top down. Employees are actively involved in the change process, whether it be adjusting production lines for new products, implementing new technologies, or refining existing processes. This high level of involvement helps to create a sense of ownership over change, which in turn reduces resistance.

Implications for the Manufacturing Industry

The findings from my research have important implications for the manufacturing industry. As product life cycles become shorter and the demand for customization increases, more manufacturing companies will need to adopt a culture of continuous change. Those that do will likely find that employee resistance to change diminishes as adaptability becomes an ingrained part of their operations. However, this shift will require not only a reevaluation of traditional change management practices, but to the quality of hiring processes too. Such companies have a precise ecosystem that can be described as natural selection. If the employee cannot deal with change, they immediately seek to exit their roles. This leaves us with the potential of a natural selection system outcome where only the fit stays. A considerable perspective to ponder.

Manufacturing companies that operate in dynamic markets will need to focus more on creating flexible, adaptive systems rather than relying on structured, formal change management processes. Leadership will remain important, but the emphasis will shift from managing change to fostering a culture of continuous improvement, empowering, trust, and innovation.

Transformational leadership among other methods of leadership remains vital in these environments, but the focus shifts from managing change to fostering innovation and resilience. The role of leadership in dynamic companies is to inspire employees to continuously improve and to ensure that the organization remains aligned with its long-term goals despite the constant state of change. This discovery opens up new avenues for research and offers valuable insights for leaders in the manufacturing industry and beyond.

The Perceived Relationship with Change Leaders and its Impact on Readiness for Change

In organizations undergoing change, the relationship between employees and their leaders or change managers is critical to the success of any change initiative. This dynamic relationship can either foster or inhibit readiness for change, depending on factors such as trust, communication, and the perceived authenticity of leadership. My research illuminated an important link between leadership and employee attitudes toward change. While the focus of my research initially centered on the leadership style and its effect on reducing resistance, it became clear that the perceived relationship between employees and change leaders played a significant role in determining the overall readiness for change. It was clear how the quality of the relationship between employees and their change leaders affected employees' openness to change. By examining trust, transparency, and empowerment within this relationship, I was able to highlight how these elements shape employees' attitudes and readiness to embrace change. Additionally, the mechanisms through which transformational leaders can strengthen their relationship with employees and thereby increase readiness for change.

The Importance of Trust in the Change Process

Trust is the foundation upon which any successful relationship between leaders and employees is built. In the context of organizational change, trust becomes even more crucial as employees look to their leaders for guidance, reassurance, and clarity during times of uncertainty. Without trust, even the most well-intentioned and thoughtfully planned change initiatives are likely to face resistance. Employees need to believe that their leaders have their best interests in mind and that the changes being introduced are necessary for the organization's long-term success. However, this will require building an organizational citizenship to begin with, and this is where I realized that this is a circular relationship that begins and ends with trust, transparency, and empowering. The degree to which employees trust their leaders has a direct impact on their readiness for change. In environments where trust is high, employees are more likely to feel confident in the direction the organization is heading and are thus more open to accepting and supporting the change process. Conversely, when trust is lacking, employees may become skeptical of leadership's motives, which can fuel resistance and increase anxiety about the future. During my research, I observed that transformational leaders who had established strong, trust-based relationships with their employees were more successful in navigating change. These leaders actively engaged with their teams, demonstrating transparency about the reasons for the change and providing regular updates on progress. In return, employees showed a higher level of commitment to the change initiatives. The employees' perception of their leaders as not only trustworthy individuals but technically savvy created a sense of psychological safety, making them more willing to take risks and embrace new ways of working.

An example of this dynamic was evident in one manufacturing company I studied. The company was undergoing a significant shift in production processes to accommodate a new product line. The CEO, who was widely regarded as a transformational leader, took the time to personally communicate with employees, explaining the rationale behind the changes and outlining how the new processes would benefit not only the company and its employees in the long run, but also the technology associated with the project. This direct engagement, combined with a history of transparent leadership, fostered trust and significantly reduced resistance to the change. Moreover, it addressed and ignited both the scientific and national spirit.

Effective communication: A Cornerstone for Building Relationships.

Effective communication is an essential component of any successful change initiative. Employees' perception of their leaders is largely shaped by how well those leaders communicate—both the rationale for change and the potential impact it will have on the organization and its employees. In the context of transformational leadership, communication is not merely about disseminating information; it is about inspiring, motivating, and aligning employees with a shared vision. It became clear that employees who felt informed and included in the change process were more likely to express readiness for change. Leaders who communicated openly, answered questions, and provided opportunities for feedback created a sense of inclusion and partnership in the change process. This transparency helped alleviate employee concerns and reduced uncertainty, which is one of the primary drivers of resistance to change.

Transformational leaders, by their nature, are effective communicators. They articulate a compelling vision for the future and ensure that employees understand their role in bringing that vision to life. This approach not only increases employee engagement but also enhances their readiness for change. Employees are more likely to embrace change when they understand the reasoning behind it and see how it aligns with the organization's broader goals.

Empowerment and Involvement in the Change Process

Employee empowerment is another key factor influencing their relationship with change managers and their readiness for change. Empowerment refers to the degree to which employees feel they have control over their work and are actively involved in the decision-making process. In the context of organizational change, empowered employees are more likely to feel a sense of ownership over the changes being introduced, which leads to higher levels of engagement and reduced resistance. I found that companies with transformational leaders who empowered their employees tended to have higher rates of change readiness. These leaders not only involved employees in the change process but also encouraged them to contribute ideas and solutions. By giving employees a voice, leaders demonstrated that they valued their input, which in turn strengthened the relationship between employees and management. An empowered workforce is more adaptable and resilient in the face of change. Employees who feel empowered are more likely to view change as an opportunity rather than a threat. This shift in perspective is crucial for fostering readiness to change. Transformational leaders play a significant role in creating an empowering environment by encouraging autonomy, providing the resources needed to succeed, and recognizing employee contributions.

The Role of Authentic Leadership in Strengthening Relationships

Authenticity in leadership is a powerful driver of trust and respect in the employee-leader relationship. Employees are more likely to follow leaders who they perceive as genuine, ethical, and aligned with the values of the organization. In the context of organizational change, authenticity helps to build credibility and reinforces the message that the change is necessary and in the best interest of both the employees and the organization. However, authenticity can only be achieved by respecting the employee's intellectuality, and there is nothing more destructive for a manager than thinking they can fake it until they make it. The employees are smarter than that and will know, and once you are caught pretending, there is nothing you can do to fix that.

Transformational leaders, by definition, are often seen as authentic because they lead with a clear sense of purpose and integrity. They are transparent about their intentions and align their actions with the values they espouse. This authenticity is critical in gaining the trust and confidence of employees during times of change.

Employees who believed their leaders were authentic were more likely to express readiness for change. Authentic leaders were seen as more approachable, and employees felt comfortable sharing their concerns without fear of retribution. This openness and vulnerability on the part of leadership created a reciprocal relationship in which employees were more willing to take risks and embrace new challenges.

An example of this was seen in a company where the leadership team made a point of being highly visible and accessible throughout the change process. The CEO regularly walked the factory floor, engaging with employees and answering questions directly. This hands-on approach not only reinforced the leader's authenticity but also created a sense of solidarity between leadership and employees. As a result, employees were more receptive to the changes being implemented and displayed a higher degree of readiness to adapt.

Impact on Organizational Readiness for Change

The relationship between employees and their leaders has a profound impact on organizational readiness for change. When employees trust their leaders, feel informed through effective communication, and are empowered to participate in the change process, their readiness to embrace change increases significantly. This readiness is essential for ensuring that change initiatives are successful and that the organization can adapt to new challenges and opportunities. Conversely, when the relationship between employees and leaders is strained—due to a lack of trust, poor communication, or disempowerment—resistance to change is likely to increase. Employees may become disengaged, skeptical, and even openly opposed to the changes being introduced. This resistance can derail change efforts and create long-lasting negative consequences for the organization. This led me to believe that transformational leadership, with its emphasis on building strong relationships with employees, is particularly effective in fostering readiness for change. By focusing on trust, communication, empowerment, and authenticity, transformational leaders create an environment where employees feel supported and motivated to embrace change.

Adaptation as the Norm

In many industries, organizational change is often met with resistance from employees who are uncomfortable with new processes, technologies, or roles. The manufacturing sector, however, particularly in companies that frequently develop new products, presents a unique environment where change is not an occasional event but a regular part of daily operations. This constant state of flux requires employees to develop adaptive mindsets, making them less prone to resisting change. In a more interesting perspective, it can be viewed as an opportunity of technical growth.

Unlike traditional industries where change initiatives are episodic and often trigger anxiety, manufacturing companies that focus on the continuous development of new products foster a work culture in which change is ingrained. This unique organizational culture, which embraces constant innovation and adaptation, leads to a workforce that is more agile and resilient when facing new challenges. In this context, employees are more likely to view change not as a disruption but as an essential part of their roles.

By exploring how the employees of manufacturing companies that consistently work on new projects are less likely to resist change because change has become a fundamental part of their working environment, we might come across astonishing findings that shed light on new areas in managing change. By examining the unique factors that contribute to this culture of adaptability, such as frequent product development, team collaboration, and the leadership approach, we may be able to unlock how companies can successfully manage change without traditional change management structures.

The Culture of Continuous Innovation

In manufacturing companies that regularly undertake new projects, whether developing new products or upgrading existing processes, change is an everyday occurrence. Employees in such environments are constantly involved in innovation cycles, from design and prototyping to production and quality control. This culture of continuous innovation creates a natural rhythm of change that employees quickly become accustomed to, reducing the likelihood of resistance. Manufacturing employees in these settings are often cross-trained in multiple skills and are encouraged to think critically about how to improve processes. This emphasis on skill versatility helps employees build confidence in their ability to adapt, reducing fear or anxiety when faced with new challenges. Rather than dreading change, they come to view it as an opportunity to enhance their competencies and contribute to the success of the company.

This type of work environment contrasts with more static industries, where employees might work on the same tasks for years and become resistant to change when it finally arrives. In dynamic manufacturing environments, however, employees are constantly exposed to new tasks and are expected to solve problems in innovative ways. As a result, their perception of change shifts from being a disruptive force to a natural progression in their roles.

One company that exemplifies this is Tesla, a leader in electric vehicle manufacturing. Tesla's frequent innovations in both product design and manufacturing processes require its employees to constantly adapt to new technologies and methods. The employees at Tesla are conditioned to expect changes, making them less likely to resist updates in processes or the introduction of new products. In fact, they are often excited about the changes because they align with the company's mission to push the boundaries of automotive engineering.

Frequent New Projects and Their Impact on Employee Mindsets

Manufacturing companies that work on multiple projects simultaneously create a fast-paced environment that demands continuous learning and adaptation. This frequency of new projects forces employees to adopt a mindset of flexibility and readiness for change. When employees are regularly involved in new projects, they become desensitized to the uncertainties associated with change, as it becomes an inherent part of their job, or it might cause fatigue for the wrong personalities that is less prone to accepting change. One key factor that reduces resistance in such environments is the regular exposure to change. Employees working on new projects are used to adjusting to different timelines, learning new systems, and collaborating with different teams. As a result, change ceases to be seen as a disruption and instead becomes part of the standard operating procedure. This frequent exposure also means that employees develop a higher level of resilience, as they are used to dealing with uncertainty and unexpected challenges.

This exposure to change creates a form of "change immunity" within the workforce. Over time, employees in such environments become so accustomed to dealing with new challenges that their tolerance for change increases significantly. In fact, they often come to see change as a necessary driver of improvement and progress rather than something to be feared or resisted. Employees in this context become proactive agents of change, contributing ideas and solutions that can help the company navigate new projects more efficiently.

For instance, at companies like Boeing, which frequently develops new aircraft models, employees must regularly adjust to new designs, materials, and production methods. Boeing employees are involved in multiple phases of a project's lifecycle, from design and engineering to manufacturing and testing, and they are accustomed to shifting priorities and project goals. The result is a workforce that is highly adaptable and less resistant to change, as they understand that innovation and evolution are essential components of their work.

Collaborative Work Environments and Change Acceptance

Another significant factor in reducing resistance to change in manufacturing companies that frequently launch new projects is the collaborative nature of the work. In such companies, teamwork and cross-functional collaboration are essential for bringing new products to market. When employees work together closely on different projects, they build strong relationships and develop a shared sense of purpose. This collective effort makes change feel less like a top-down directive and more like a shared responsibility.

Collaboration plays a crucial role in fostering openness to change because it involves the sharing of ideas, knowledge, and resources across departments. When employees feel that they are part of a larger team working towards a common goal, they are more likely to embrace change as a necessary step to achieving success. This sense of unity helps to diminish resistance, as employees feel that they are contributing to the change rather than being passive recipients of it.

In manufacturing settings, collaborative environments also encourage continuous feedback loops, where employees can voice their concerns, provide input, and suggest improvements. This involvement gives them a sense of ownership over the change process, making them more likely to support and champion new initiatives. Additionally, leaders in these environments tend to practice more inclusive leadership styles, such as transformational leadership, which focuses on inspiring and motivating teams to embrace change as a pathway to success.

A case in point is Toyota, which employs the Kaizen philosophy of continuous improvement in its manufacturing processes. At Toyota, employees across all levels of the organization are encouraged to contribute ideas on how to improve production efficiency, quality, and safety. This emphasis on collaboration ensures that change is viewed positively, as employees see it as a natural outcome of their contributions and problem-solving efforts. Toyota's collaborative culture has helped it become one of the most innovative and adaptable companies in the automotive industry, with employees who are not only open to change but actively seek it out.

Leadership's Role in Cultivating Change-Ready Employees

Leadership plays a pivotal role in shaping employee attitudes toward change whether in selecting, training, cultivating, and supporting. In manufacturing companies that work on constant new projects, leaders must model adaptability and encourage a culture of openness to change. Transformational leadership, which emphasizes vision, inspiration, and empowerment, is particularly effective in environments where change is frequent.

Transformational leaders create an atmosphere where employees feel supported and motivated to take on new challenges. They focus on building trust, promoting innovation, and fostering a shared vision of the future. By clearly communicating the reasons for change and involving employees in the decision-making process, transformational leaders reduce the fear and uncertainty that often accompany change initiatives. In manufacturing companies with constantly evolving projects, leaders act as change agents, guiding their teams through transitions and ensuring that they have the resources and support they need to succeed. When employees trust their leaders and feel confident in their ability to navigate change, they are less likely to resist it. This trust is built through transparent communication, regular feedback, and recognition of employee contributions to the company's success.

For example, at General Electric (GE), a company known for its continuous innovation across multiple industries, leaders play a key role in fostering a change-ready culture. GE's leadership development programs emphasize adaptability and encourage leaders to be proactive in managing change. As a result, GE employees are trained to view change as an opportunity for growth, both personally and professionally, making them more likely to embrace new projects and initiatives.

The Benefits of a Change-Accepting Workforce

The ability of manufacturing employees to adapt quickly to new projects and changes brings significant benefits to both the organization and the workforce. For the organization, a change-accepting culture leads to higher productivity, faster innovation, and a more agile response to market demands. Companies that can quickly pivot and implement new ideas have a competitive advantage, especially in industries where technological advancements and consumer preferences evolve rapidly.

For employees, working in an environment where change is the norm leads to personal growth and professional development. Employees become more versatile, enhancing their skills and expanding their knowledge base. This adaptability not only makes them more valuable to their current employer but also prepares them for future career opportunities.

Moreover, when employees are accustomed to change, they experience less stress and anxiety when new initiatives are introduced. Rather than fearing the unknown, they approach change with confidence, knowing that they have successfully navigated similar challenges in the past. This resilience creates a more positive and dynamic workplace environment, where innovation and progress are embraced rather than resisted. This change-accepting culture benefits both the organization and its employees, fostering a dynamic environment where adaptability and innovation thrive. By understanding how constant change influences employee mindsets, other industries can learn valuable lessons about how to reduce resistance to change and create more resilient, agile organizations.

In Concussion

Organizational change is a vital process aimed at solving problems or enhancing goods and services to maintain corporate sustainability and competitive advantage. Typically, change initiatives begin with high enthusiasm at the management level but can encounter resistance when communication between change managers and employees is ineffective. This lack of communication not only affects the relationship between managers and their teams but also fosters peer resistance.

Aside from introducing a new process or technology, one significant area requiring extensive change management and communication is during partnerships, mergers, and acquisitions. In such cases, cultural differences between businesses create complexity and resistance. Meticulous communication is crucial to ensure alignment and success. The high failure rate of mergers and partnerships underscores the importance of selecting the right leaders to manage these sensitive changes. There is no universally prescribed leadership style, as different leaders exhibit varied behaviors and traits depending on the circumstances.

The question remains: Can one leadership style effectively reduce employee resistance to change? It is likely that leaders who can turn resistance into momentum may be successful, though context is crucial.

Change managers often find themselves overwhelmed by issues such as funding, milestones, and team dynamics, which can lead to communication breakdowns and increased resistance. Given the complexity of organizational change, it becomes critical for companies to select leaders with the right skills to manage change effectively. Many business leaders in the manufacturing industry ask how they can determine which leadership style is best suited for their teams during periods of change. However, it is also important to hire the right personalities for the right position. The research found that transformational leadership—marked by traits like individual consideration and intellectual stimulation—creates an environment of trust and communication that reduces resistance to change. Leaders who empower employees and foster a sense of shared purpose are more likely to succeed in guiding their teams through change. However, not to disregard the personal employees' traits at the earlier stages of recruitment, training, and cultivation, and most importantly not to disregard whether or not the organization is dynamic by nature or not.

www.ingramcontent.com/pod-product-compliance
Lightning Source LLC
Chambersburg PA
CBHW070958220526
45471CB00007B/3089